Madge Kendal

The Drama

A paper read at the congress of the national association for the promotion

of social science, Birmingham, Sept., 1884

Madge Kendal

The Drama
A paper read at the congress of the national association for the promotion of social science, Birmingham, Sept., 1884

ISBN/EAN: 9783337034948

Printed in Europe, USA, Canada, Australia, Japan

Cover: Foto ©Suzi / pixelio.de

More available books at **www.hansebooks.com**

BY

Mrs. KENDAL

*A PAPER READ AT THE CONGRESS
OF THE NATIONAL ASSOCIATION FOR THE
PROMOTION OF SOCIAL SCIENCE,
BIRMINGHAM, SEPTEMBER 1884*

LONDON
DAVID BOGUE, 3 ST. MARTIN'S PLACE,
TRAFALGAR SQUARE

THE DRAMA.

IN dealing with the Drama within the necessarily brief limits of a Social Science Association paper, the great difficulty is to decide from what point of view so large a subject is to be treated. That it should have a place in your discussions seems appropriate enough, for assuredly there never was a time when the Theatre was more popular, or so much a topic of conversation, as now. The English people are indeed rapidly becoming alive to the fact that the "progress and culture of a nation depend upon its diversions as well as upon its occupations," and as a matter of consequence the Dramatic Art is receiving an unprecedented meed of recognition. It appears to me, therefore, that the most useful thing for me to do to-day will be to glance for a few moments at the

B

difference in the condition of the Drama in its earliest days and now, and to consider in what ways it has improved, in what deteriorated.   That it has in many ways improved, every playgoer of intelligence must admit ; that it has in some ways deteriorated, those who are closely associated with it are forced to allow.

It is an easy and a pleasant task to speak of its improvements.   I believe—nay, I know—that there still exist very worthy but self-constituted critics who speak with shake of head and regretful sigh of what are called the " palmy days " of the Drama. That grand actors and consummate actresses lived in bygone days is a matter beyond all dispute ; and indeed when one comes to consider the conditions under which they were compelled to follow their art, it seems almost impossible to speak too highly of the genius which enabled them indelibly to stamp their names upon the age in which they lived, and which will cause them to be honourably—nay, gloriously—remembered in ages yet to come.   But surely I am justified in saying that the playgoer of to-day possesses advantages far and away above those which his forefathers enjoyed. Let us compare for a moment the playhouses of which we read with those with which we are familiar.

In the old days the utmost disorder was allowed to exist in the half-lighted auditorium. Eating and drinking were freely indulged in ; smoking was permitted ; wine, spirits, and tobacco were hawked about ; card-playing was resorted to between the acts; the more distinguished among the audience were allowed to walk and sit on the stage, and to converse with the performers. It was no disgrace in those days for gentlemen of good social position to be seen tipsy at the play, and of course drunken brawls and disgraceful quarrels were of frequent occurrence.

The entertainment provided on the stage was on a level with the intellect of the audience, and the playgoers were looked upon as "rogues and vagabonds." No wonder that the Drama got a bad name, or that people with a Puritanical turn of mind regarded it with dismay.

Of course all this is going back a very long way, and matters began by degrees to improve ; but I venture to say that it was not until the present generation that correctness in costume, fidelity in scene-painting, and attention to every little detail con-

nected with the action, came to be looked
upon as absolutely essential to the proper
production of a play.

Nowadays, indeed, that which is techni-
cally known as the " staging " of a play is
in itself a work of true art, and in its own
way gives rise to as much thought and care
as the author has for his dialogue or the
actor for his part. It has been objected
lately that too much attention is apt to be
given to scenery, furniture, and accessories,
and that there is a danger of the Drama
suffering from over-elaboration in this
direction. In plain English, this means a
thing may be too well done ; and it seems
hard to subscribe to such a theory. Our
forefathers, you will remember, were content with a background for their plays on
which the name of the place supposed to
be represented was written up, such as—
" This is Thebes," or " This is a forest ; "
or sometimes even this trouble was not
taken, and the actors had to inform the
audience where the action of the piece lay.

" Our scene is Rhodes,"

is the brilliant opening line given to an
actor in an old drama.

These crude arrangements gave way to
the introduction of scenery, but it was a

long time before anything like correctness was attempted, and we can most of us remember the days when there was no complaint of the thing being "overdone." Can it be "overdone"? If a scene is to be represented at all, can it be given with too much truth or attention to detail? Of course, lack of judgment spoils everything, and it is very likely that mistakes in this direction have given rise to the complaint. It is useless to lavish mere money on a scene. If the interior of a peasant's cottage is to be represented, much expenditure on the furniture would be ridiculous; but surely the artistic care that reproduces the humble home of the labourer, down to such minute details as, say, the "sampler" stitched in silk which his wife had worked when a girl at the village school, and which now decorates his walls, is a thing to be admired.

Again, if the scene is a landscape, ought it not to be made as true to lovely nature as the resources of art will allow? Or if it is a room in a palace, can it be too beautifully given? If the surroundings and *minutiæ* of such scenes are correct and in good taste, they must add not only to the enjoyment, but to the *education* of an audience; for it may be reasonably supposed that the

frequenters of the less expensive seats in a
theatre have not many opportunities of becoming familiar with the interiors of palaces;
and it is certain that the jaded City clerk,
who seeks a little recreation at the play,
does not see too much of landscape, nor has
he a very intimate acquaintance with the in-
describable attractions of an English vil-
lager's home.   Perhaps it would be well
for those who are disposed to be satirical
concerning what they call "over-attention
to detail" and "over-elaboration," to give
a thought to this side of the question before
airing their opinions.

It may then, I think, be conceded that
in matters of scenery the improvements are
not only great but remarkable.

The comfort of the audience, too—is not
that considered nowadays as it was never
considered before ?   For obvious reasons I
do not often form one of an audience my-
self, but I should certainly think that good
light, attention to warmth and ventilation,
soft cushions. ample room, good music, and,
above all cleanliness, are things to be appreciated and to be added to our list of
improvements.

And while advances in this respect have
been made before the curtain, equally great

ones have taken place behind it, and actors
and actresses are at last surrounded by the
conveniences and comforts which gentlemen
and ladies have a right to expect.   For the
improvements—the great improvements—
that have been made in this way honour
should be given where honour is due.   It
was the Management of the Prince of
Wales Theatre that, some seventeen years
ago, first paid attention to the comfort of
the artists it engaged, and made the theatre
behind the scenes what it now is.   This
fact should be recorded, because praise is
too often given to those who have only
followed a good example.

We have more play-writers, too, than of
old ; and although a cry is constantly going
up that there is a dearth of good dramatists,
it is a matter of fact that much excellent
modern literary work has been, and is,
associated with the Stage.

It is to be feared that the playwright of
to-day is hardly appreciated as he should
be.   His work is subject to keen and universal criticism ; for it is a curious fact,
that whereas few would venture to criticize
books, poems, or paintings without some
little special knowledge, every one thinks
he has a right to pronounce judgment on a

stage-play, and is convinced that that judgment is infallible. And, again, the dra-
matist runs the risk of being misinterpreted,
and consequently misunderstood. His work,
moreover, does not find its place on the
library shelf, and is seldom read ; but the
improved condition of the Theatre has
made the most famous literary men of the
day anxious to identify their names with it ;
and let us hope that this desire will increase
and bring forth good fruit as matters still
further improve.

But perhaps the most remarkable change
that has come over the condition of the
Drama is the fact that there is at last a
recognised social position for the professional player. Formerly actors formed a
little body in themselves. The Theatrical
Profession was considered outside, if not
beneath, all others, and was regarded with
something like contempt. It was a wrong,
a cruel, and an absurd state of things, for
even then the Theatre was popular, and
was doing good work. Perhaps you may
remember Garrick's famous reply to the
Bishop, who told him that he could not
understand why his theatre was always full
while his church was always empty. "I
think, my Lord," said Garrick, "it is

because I deal with fiction as though it were a truth, while you preaeh a truth as though it were a fiction." Members of all the other professions were glad enough to come and amuse themselves with the outcome of the actor's genius ; his ability was recognised ; it was, as it is now, the subject of universal conversation and of much newspaper comment ; but the door of " society" was closed to him. Now all that is altered. The Theatrical Profession is acknowledged to be a high and important one, and the society of the intelligent and cultivated actor is eagerly sought after. Just at present, indeed, the new state of things, having become universally known and recognised, has become also a little embarrassing.

One is always hearing or reading in the papers that the professions are "overstocked "—that there aro too many clergymen, too many lawyers, too many doctors, and the fact that the terms of actor and of gentleman may now be regarded as synonymous, seems to have sent the "overdraft" of all these other professions headlong on to the stage.

How many younger sons of well-born but not too well-to-do parents have hailed the present social position of the actor with

delight? How many educated girls, find-
ing themselves, through force of circum-
stances, suddenly compelled to face the
world on their own account, have turned
with a sigh of relief from the prospect of
the stereotyped position of "companion,"
or "governess" to the vista that an honourable connection with the Stage holds out
to them? From these, and from other
sources, the Theatrical Profession also runs
the risk of becoming "over-stocked."

These young aspirants rush to the Stage
as to a promised land. The would-be
actors congratulate themselves on the fact
that there are no "stiff" examinations to
pass; they complacently regard their hand-
some young faces in the looking-glass; they
contemplate with satisfaction the latest
efforts of their West-end tailors, and think
themselves on the high-road to fame and
fortune.

A young man of this stamp not long ago
called upon a London manager, sent in his
card, and being admitted to his presence,
informed him that he had made up his
mind to "go on the stage," and was prepared to accept an engagement. The
manager, not unnaturally, asked some
questions as to his qualifications for the
career which he proposed for himself.

"Had he any experience as an actor? Had he studied the dramatic art?" "No," was the reply, "but he had decided to 'go on the stage,' and all that he wanted was an engagement." The manager led him to the door, and, returning his card, pointed to a building on the opposite side of the street. "That," said he, "is a bank; go and present yourself there. Say that, without knowing anything about the business, you have made up your mind to be a banker's clerk, and ask for a situation. If you succeed in getting one, come back here and I will engage you as an actor." The young gentleman took his departure, but *he did not return!*

The would-be actresses are more diffident, and are certainly more disposed to devote heart and soul to their work; but neither the one nor the other has the slightest idea of the amount of study, of labour, and of devotion to the art—to say nothing of natural aptitude—that is necessary for success.

Another advance that may be claimed for the Drama in these days of its improvement is its influence as a teacher— for a teacher it always has been, and ever will be.

Temperaments differ everywhere, and
one of the first things that a boy or girl
has to find out is what will exercise the
greatest influence over his or her nature.
There are many young people who are
perfectly content and happy with the
amusements that are afforded by study, by
a happy home life, and by pleasant social
intercourse ; but there are also many who
require a little more than this, and who can
only show what is best in their undeveloped
natures under the influence of an appeal to
their imaginations. These rush to the
Drama as the thirsty wayfarer rushes to the
cooling brooklet.

How important it is, therefore, that the
draught should be pure, that the refresh-
ment should be really wholesome and useful. It is quite certain that many hundreds
—nay, thousands—of people have been influenced for good or for evil by what they
have seen portrayed upon the stage. Those
who go to the theatre with the capability of
weeping over scenes in which honest self-
sacrifice is depicted ; of being aroused to
enthusiasm over the success of manly effort
or womanly devotion ; or of feeling genuine
contempt for the portrayal of meanness,
treachery, and snobbery, will come away
from a good play, well acted, having learnt

a lesson and gained an experience that will probably be remembered with advantage throughout the remainder of their lives. A pure Stage is likely to be surrounded by a pure people, and its influence from this point of view can hardly be over-estimated.

It is worth while here, perhaps, to look upon the influence that the Dramatic Art has upon those most intimately associated with it. The playing of many parts naturally gives to the actor and actress a curious insight into the sentiments and passions that sway and bias human nature. The earnest actor, who has heart and soul in his work, and conscientiously studies the various parts he is called upon to play, is compelled to think, more than the mere man of business, of human strength and weakness, of hate and love, of joy and sorrow; for in their turn he has to portray them all, and, to judge by results, the effect upon his nature is to make him very charitable.

Where, I may safely ask, is charity more openly or more cheerfully practised than among the members of the Theatrical Profession? I do not allude to mere almsgiving—the readiness with which an actor will in that way help a comrade who has

C

fallen by the way has become proverbial ; but to charity of a very different and more valuable kind.

Clergymen preach forgiveness, but they do not welcome among their own body men whose names are identified with a stormy past, but who would gladly do useful work in a peaceful future. Lawyers have to do with justice, but they look with wary eye on those who have once tripped, and conscientiously warn their clients to have nothing to do with such easily misled and consequently dangerous creatures. Doctors practise the healing art, but their nostrums are for broken bones and bodily hurts ; they have no salve for the weary mind or the lacerated heart.

The Theatrical Profession, on the other hand, offers chances to all men and women, no matter what their past has been ; and it is in this way that I maintain it to be a more charitable one than any other. A sad and undeserved consequence of this is, that actors are liable to suffer as a body for the very charities they so unselfishly practise, for they give the outside world opportunities of indulging in that scandal about the Stage which apparently forms one of its chief delights. The Puritanical-minded point to some too well-known " backslider " who

is endeavouring to earn a living in a theatre,
lift up their pious hands in horror, and condemn the whole profession.   It would be
well, indeed, if these worthy people would
take the trouble to look a little further into
the matter, and ascertain how cruelly unjust such condemnation is.

In all these things—and if time permitted
I could mention many more—the Drama,
it may be safely maintained, has not only
held its ground, but improved.   But I am
now quite half-way through the time allotted
by the Social Science Association for my
paper, and I must turn to the other side of
the question, and tell you in what ways the
Drama of the present day has deteriorated,
and, unless actors and actresses will be true
to themselves and the honourable profession
that they follow, is likely still further to
deteriorate.

No true lover of the Dramatic Art can
look with satisfaction on the many ways in
which it is now advertised.   Neither the
painter nor the poet thinks it advisable to
fill the columns of the daily papers with
the monotonous repetition of what this or
that critic has said of his work, or to keep
his name constantly, and with wearisome

persistency, before the public. The extent to which some carry out this system, and the pains taken over it, is simply beyond all description. An insatiable thirst for newspaper paragraphs is always tormenting them, and in every action of their lives the thought of "How will that advertise me?" or, "How can I use this as an advertisement?" is predominant. With people thus constituted, even affliction is turned to what they consider profitable account, and at a dull period an illness is regarded as a positive boon.

This absurd mania seems to be in a great measure, I am sorry to say, peculiar to the members of the Theatrical Profession, and it assuredly does not add to their dignity. It is done in manifold ways—in what are known as "receptions" at theatres, in railway station "demonstrations," by photography, and by speech-making, and one and all are degrading to the Drama. As a cloak for incapability such means may be excusable, but true art in every branch advertises itself. Advertising nowadays is an art, but it is *not* the art of Acting.

This state of things has given rise to a flippant and what may be termed "personal" style of theatrical journalism, which is greatly to be deplored, and should cer-

tainly be discouraged. The so-called theatrical papers, in which the leading artists of
the stage are alluded to by their Christian
names, and where insolent and generally
untrue gossip and tittle-tattle take the
place of honest criticism, are absolutely
debasing to the profession. The unfortunate
outcome of all this is, that the artist's capability, or, more properly speaking, "popu-
larity," is too often gauged by the amount
of publicity that is given to every little
action of his or her life. An unthinking
section of the public is hungry for news
of this description, and incompetent but
"knowing" actors and their managers
take advantage of it.

Another way in which the Drama has
certainly deteriorated is the style of play
that now attracts popular audiences. Our
forefathers could laugh heartily over a good
farce, but the staple fare of the evening had
to be the serious or poetical Drama, in
which some good moral would be pointed
out, and literary merit would be looked for
and found. At the present time, however,
audiences enjoy a whole evening of farce,
and farce of a very remarkable nature?
What, in reality, can be a more painful
spectacle than that of an innocent and un-

suspecting wife being hoodwinked and deceived by a graceless and profligate husband? Years ago it would have formed the groundwork of a very pathetic play, if not of a tragedy; but now it is a never-failing source of delight to the lover of elongated farce; and the greater the inno-cence of the wife, and the more outrageous the misconduct of the husband, the louder are the shrieks of laughter with which their misunderstandings are received.

For this, alas! we have to thank our French friends; and the "suggestiveness" which pervades the dialogue of too many modern plays is another foreign importa-tion that might very well be spared. That most of the old plays were indelicate is a matter of fact, but they were a reflection of the times in which they were produced. In those days a spade was called a spade, and plain speaking was not only tolerated but expected. That disagreeable "sugges-tion" should have taken the place of down-right coarseness is a bad sign of the taste of the modern playgoer. Of course there are very clever and very amusing pieces of this order, but their success has given rise to a host of vulgar and clumsy imitations, which, while attracting audiences, certainly do no credit to the English stage.

In what is known as burlesque, too, the modern Theatre has decidedly deteriorated. Genuine travesty and pantomime are distinct and recognized branches of the Dramatic Art ; but though some good burlesque pieces, in which witty authors and clever actors unite to create a hearty, wholesome, and good-humoured laugh, are happily produced from time to time, the so-called burlesque with which the modern playgoer is familiar, and which, it must be owned, he seems to enjoy, is not a very high-toned entertainment. I am sure that if fanciful children were taken to these pieces, it would be a real source of sorrow to them to see such trusted friends as " Ali Baba," " Aladdin," " Robin Hood," " Robinson Crusoe," " Sinbad the Sailor," and a host of others, treated so badly.

No one in his senses can blame managers or actors for catering for this section of the play-going public. A demand naturally induces a supply, and if Dramatic Art has deteriorated in this direction, the public, and not the profession, is to blame.

I do not think that the Press of the present day does all that it might do for the true welfare of the Drama. Existing critics generally rush into extremes, and either

over-praise or too cruelly condemn. The
public, as a matter of course, turns to the
newspapers for information. And how can
any judgment be formed when either indis-
criminate praise or unqualified abuse is
given to almost every new piece that is
brought out? Criticism, if it is to be worth
anything, should surely be "criticism";
but nowadays the writing of a picturesque
article, replete with eulogy or the reverse,
seems to be the aim of the theatrical re-
viewer.

Of course the influence of the Press upon
the Stage is very powerful, but it will cease
to be so if playgoers find that their
mentors, the critics, are not trustworthy
guides. The public, after all, must decide
the fate of a new play. If it be bad, the
Englishman of to-day will not declare that
it is good because the newspapers have
told him so. He will be disappointed, he
will be bored, he will tell his friends, and
the bad piece will fail to draw audiences.

If, on the other hand, the play is a good
one, which has been condemned by the
Press, it will quicken the pulse and stir the
heart of an audience in spite of adverse
criticism; the report that it contains the
true ring will go about, and success must
follow. In a word, though the Press can

do very much to further the interests of the
Stage, it is powerless to kill good work,
and it cannot galvanize that which is in-
vertebrate into life. Too many notices are,
it is to be feared, written "to order," and
the writer who has declined to praise an
unsuccessful actor has been known to lose
his post; but let us hope that this unjust
state of affairs, together with the "chicken
and champagne," of which we have heard
so much, is a thing of the past.

And here, I think, attention may be suit-
ably called to a duty that the public undoubtedly owes to itself in this matter of
criticism, and that is, that it should judge for
itself, and not pin a blind faith on all that
is told it. It is too true that if playgoers
are told that a thing is good they are quite
prepared to accept it as such, without tak-
ing the trouble to find out whether they
have been rightly or wrongly informed.
Thus many plays and many actors and
actresses are accepted and praised because
the critics have declared them to be good.
The fact is, the public does not judge
for itself, but is influenced and led by
"fashion."

Actors nowadays seem to be judged by
everything except by the art they follow,

and I maintain that this state of things
is peculiar to the Theatrical Profession.
Clergymen become popular because they
preach good sermons ; lawyers have large
practices because they advise their clients
well ; doctors increase the number of their
patients in proportion to their professional
skill ; surely then actors should be suc-
cessful and popular in accordance with the
talent with which they act. But Acting
seems to have something akin to "Parr's
Life Pills" and "Holloway's Ointment."
By advertising those commodities large for-
tunes were made, and it is the actor who
lets the public know, through the newspapers, everything that he does, from the
entertainments that he gives to his friends
and admirers, down to the goose that he
sends his gasman at Christmas, that seems
to get the largest following. "Bunkum"
of this description has of late years been
practised to an extent which is absolutely
nauseating ; and all this proves that there
is

"Something rotten in the state of Denmark."

A complaint is constantly being made
that the moral tone of the Drama of the
present day is not so high as it undoubtedly
should be ; but for this playgoers are to

blame, for they run after notoriety, and notoriety alone. This may seem a strong accusation, but is it not true? When men and women have done wrong and take to the Stage, is it not a fact that (provided the wrong-doing has been made sufficiently public) brisk business may be expected at the booking office? This, I maintain, never was in the old days, and proves to-day the degradation of our Stage.

Some critics hold that men and women cannot properly act noble and virtuous characters unless they themselves have led spotless lives. I do not go so far as this, but I do maintain that it is pleasanter to think that when the curtain has fallen, and the actor or actress is at home, he or she leads, or is capable of leading, the same kind of life the representation of which has moved an audience to sympathetic tears; and certainly it can be no drawback if, while admiring the artist, the playgoer can at the same time respect the man or woman.

Surely, then, it is more than a necessity that actors and actresses of position, who have the true interest of their noble art in view, should make their lives an example to those with whom they are associated, and to those who are to come after them.

By this means, and by this means only, can the Theatrical Profession expect to maintain its dignity and to secure the high position it should hold in the estimation of the public. It behoves actors and actresses of every degree, while cultivating their talents to elevate and amuse, to lead such lives that those who have regarded the Stage with a suspicious eye will at last give it its proper place in the world of Art.

Time will not allow me to say more. The Drama has an interesting, nay, to some of us a fascinating, Past. It rests with those who make it a profession, and the ever-increasing public that supports it, to secure for it a useful, an elevating, and a glorious Future.

BALLANTYNE PRESS, CHANDOS STREET, W.C.

A LIST OF WORKS

RELATING TO

THE DRAMA AND MUSIC

PUBLISHED BY

MR. DAVID BOGUE.

www.ingramcontent.com/pod-product-compliance
Lightning Source LLC
Chambersburg PA
CBHW021458090426
42739CB00009B/1783